Return to Inanna

Also by Christine Irving:

Be a Teller of Tales

The Naked Man

You Can Tell A Crone By Her Cackle

Sitting on the Hag Seat: A Celtic Knot of Poems

Magdalene A.D.

The Mystery of the Black Madonna (Juvenile literature)

A Rose in Winter (A 3-act play written in collaboration
with poet Kathryn Smith)

Motorcycle Dreaming: Riding the 'Beauty Way'
Back in Time Across America

Celtic Wheel of the Year

Return to Inanna

Christine Irving

Aurochs Press
Denton, Texas

Christine Irving

chrsrvng5@gmail.com

http://www.christineirving.com/

Ordering Information:

Quantity sales: Special discounts are available on quantity purchases by corporations, associations, and others.

For details, contact the publisher at the address above.

Orders by U.S. trade bookstores and wholesalers.

Please contact:

chrsrvng5@gmail.com

Printed in the United States of America

Publisher's Cataloging-in-Publication data

Irving, Christine

Return to Inanna / Christine Irving

p. cm.

ISBN 9781790983896

1. The main category of the book —Poetry — Other category.
2. Myth. 3. Spirituality. 4. Women's issues. 5 Feminism.

First Edition

14 13 12 11 10 / 10 9 8 7 6 5 4 3 2 1

Book cover - Designed and illustrated by Christine Irving

Acknowledgments

Undying thanks to my beloved husband John, proofreader, editor and sounding board par excellence.

I am also grateful to my poetry critique group Beth Honeycutt, J. Paul Holcomb and Robert Schinzel whose wise and helpful suggestions not only keep me honest, but immeasurably enrich the work.

Thanks also go to novelist and playwright Shay Youngblood and poet Kelly Weathers for reading the manuscript in whole and offering their wise and useful critiques.

I am indebted to the many, many women with whom I have sat in circle and shared ritual. Special thanks go to Mary Greer and Sharyn MacDonald for teaching me so much about how to create, conduct and participate in ritual.

In memory of the Honorable Olivia Robertson, founding mother of the Fellowship of Isis, who ordained me Priestess and inspired me to study the art of ritual and sacred theater.

Christine Irving

Table of Contents

Part I

Tablets of Enheduanna's poetry:

Enheduanna (2285-2250 BCE) first known author
and poet in written history, high priestess to
Inanna, and daughter of Akkadian/Sumerian king,
Sargon the Great.

Enheduanna Imprisoned

Torn from Inanna's temple, her priestess paces
tracking damp footprints across the tiled floor.
Sweat trickles down the supple spine,
drips between pomegranate breasts,
beads in tiny pearls above her upper lip.

Lady Enheduanna shimmers in lamplight,
a radiating nimbus of concentrated fury.
Outside the bronze-hinged door a soldier coughs.
Arms rattle, muffled passwords mark
the moon's pale progress,
shadows play across a wall…

Lady squats beside her scribe
whispering fiercely.
Stylus scratches clay.

Night by night the paean unwinds…

Return to Inanna

Gist of the Myth

Long ago and far away in the Land of Ur, Inanna Queen of Heaven, rules as goddess of love and war. It's a lot for one deity to reconcile within herself – tenderness and ruthlessness, forgiveness and revenge. As you'll see, it's complicated.

Inanna possesses seven powers, known as the *me*, which she acquired from her father Enki through trickery. Each power manifests as a physical item worn or carried by Inanna. She is thought by her family of gods to be inordinately ambitious. They suspect her of coveting the powers of the nether kingdom belonging to her sister Ereshkigal, Queen of the Underworld.

Ereshkigal and Inanna have history. Lusty Inanna once desired a beautiful young shepherd who spurned her for a man. Furious at the insult, she begged her brother Utu, the sun god, to let his ferocious Bull of Heaven rampage and destroy the pasture lands, but the shepherd and his boyfriend battled the bull and killed him. As with so many mythic creatures, the bull had an alternate form. He was husband to Ereshkigal.

Whatever Inanna's true agenda – whether to console the widow or steal her might – the goddess determines to go underground and visit her sister. Girding herself in her seven powers she takes off alone. Before Inanna leaves, she tells Ninshubar, her handmaiden, what to do if she does not return.

When Inanna comes calling, Ereshkigal orders seven gates placed across the only road in and out of her kingdom, all of them too narrow for a horse and chariot. The first gate opens wide enough for a man in armor to walk through, but each gate thereafter shrinks a little as walls compress, lintels lower and thresholds rise. At each gate, Neti the gatekeeper accosts her, demanding one of her powers in return for passage.

Meanwhile Ereshkigal, suffering a latent prolonged labor with her dead husband's child, never ceases wailing. Her inconsolable grief is interfering with the birth process.

When Inanna, stripped of clothing, crawls through the seventh gate onto the floor of a great hall she gets to her feet, tosses her unbound hair and saunters naked towards the throne. Ereshkigal rises to greet her, but Inanna plunks herself down on the empty seat. No sooner has she set bare bottom to stone than seven judges file in. Their judgement is quick and its execution quicker. Within minutes Inanna is struck dead and her body hung on a meat hook.

Up above, in the land of Ur, faithful Ninshubar follows Inanna's directions. She waits for three days before mourning in the prescribed manner, then runs from god to god, seeking aid for her mistress. The gods ignore her pleas until she approaches Enki, Lord of the Earth, who agrees to help and creates two entities called the *gala*. To one he gives a life-giving plant, to the other he gives the water of life. Enki tells his creatures to sneak past the gates and seek out Ereshkigal, listen to her laments and mourn with her.

Ereshkigal, comforted by being heard, recommences labor. She offers the *gala* a reward and they bargain for Inanna's body. The *gala* sprinkle the miraculous water and plant across the corpse, restoring her to life. But the seven judges are not pleased, they demand a body for a body. Inanna, accompanied by a posse of demons, returns through the seven gates, one-by-one regaining her surrendered powers. Together, she and her demonic guards go in search of a substitute.

Ninshubar begs to take her place, but Inanna refuses the offer. The search continues as they visit Inanna's son Lulal and her hairdresser Cara, find them in deep mourning and press on. Finally, they come to Inanna's lover Dumuzi and find him taking his ease beneath an apple tree, barely aware of her absence. Hurt and furious, Inanna orders the demons to grab Dumuzi, but he makes a run for it.

Weeks later, when they finally track him down, his sister Geshtinana begs to take his place. Perhaps Inanna is moved to pity. Perhaps, she misses her lover and doesn't care to lose him completely. In the end, Dumuzi goes underground for half of each year while his sister substitutes for him during the remaining six months. This, the storytellers say, is how summer and winter came to be.

PART 1

The Myth
5,000 BCE

Return to Inanna

Evening and Morning
She Shines in the Heavens

... like the nameless poor, you wear only a single garment.
The pearls of a prostitute are placed around your neck,
and you are likely to snatch a man from the tavern.
~ Simon Fiore trans., *Voices From The Clay*

Fresh lit at dusk she blazes.
She is the evening star,
daughter of the moon
dancing into darkness.

Beautiful naked Inanna
leads the stars in merry rounds.
Wearing a necklace of pearls
she sways like a tavern girl
dancing on a table.

Reborn from darkness
she is the morning star,
sister to the sun,
rising into brightness.

Nanna's calf, she sets her sight
upon the tip of mother's silver horn,
follows close behind her hoofs
learning paths of light and shadow.

She is youngest of the young,
oldest of the old. The destroyer,
the maker, the sacred, the profane;
lewd and chaste, fierce in war and play,
contrary, enigmatic to all others,
never to herself.

Inanna,
daughter of the moon,
sister to the sun,
seeking her own sacrifice,
devising her own return.

Her Sister's Voice

Dry ground trembles, pebbles jump.
Earth ruptures rent by thrusting fist
tight-clenched round wicked talons,
razor-honed to grasp and tear.

Owl wrenches free,
serrated velvet feathers bite the air.
Unwinding gyre by gyre
he spirals moonward. From below
Ereshkigal's harsh voice shouts orders:

> *Bring me a willful woman –*
> *a lusty fool and sage,*
> *regal, humble, fierce –*
> *one who knows the stories*
> *who tells the tales. Tell her:*

> *Time has reached its fullness…*

> *Split the pomegranate,*
> *crush the ripe red seed*
> *between your teeth –*
> *let the juice, bittersweet,*
> *drip honey-venom into every vein.*

> *Life and death will fight for you.*
> *Surrender to their outcome*
> *without prayer, without hope…*

Entangled

I had a sister,
silent in the womb,
who curled her thumb into my mouth
and sucked on mine.

I ate her.
Molecule by molecule,
absorbed into my skin
her body gave up sustenance
for mine. Unwittingly I dined,
accepting life.

Her lot was death.

But still she lives as shadow,
poor lost soul, wandering bodiless
through Stygian fields and gloomy
justice halls devoid of color, mirth or play.

Though waking I know her not,
she haunts my dreams, dims every joy
with undefined regret, wails my name,
the only word she knows,
calling like a loon until my ears
bleed with her keening.

I will descend.
Brave the seven gates and guards,
seek her out through dusky passageways,
search the dreary throne room,
sit in her seat and face her judges.

Queens never beg for mercy.

The Hairdresser

Cara is my singer, my manicurist and my hairdresser.
~ The Electronic Text Corpus of Sumerian Literature

Cara pouts, snaps his scissors.
Angry click-clicks punctuate each snip.
Inanna, missing the rhythmic chirp
of contented Cara, sweet cricket boy,
flamboyant prankster, trusted confidant,
glances askance to check his hands -
rock steady, bent upon her bidding.

She nods, returns to gauging odds,
each facet of her schema turned upside down,
flipped vertically and scanned for flaws.

"Done!"
Cara stoops beside his queen.

Cheek to jowl, owl-eyed,
they gaze like graven images
into a disk of burnished brass –
deep-set eyes, heavy brows, amber skin
mark them kin. He holds her hand,
files nails to spear points, paints them
scarlet as a setting sun.

"If I die tonight, what will you do?"

Rosy cloud rumbles,
lightning streaks the turquoise sky.

"Kill?" questions Cara.

"Mourn," Inanna answers…
"Wait."

Inanna to Her Lions

Inanna sits on harnessed lions…
~ The Electronic Text Corpus of Sumerian Literature

Go now, my Beauties.
Do not flatten ears and hiss.
Turn those mournful eyes aside,
you may not follow.

Your lives depend on sunlight.
Where I go, it does not shine
and you who carried me like a cub,
licked my milky face, nipped gently
when I toddled off too far,
would fade to shadows.

You eat from my hand
and share my marriage bed.
Your caterwauling
screams across the battlefield
scattering my foes. I do not forget.
But this I do alone.

Look how my golden breastplate gleams!
You've seen it turn a thousand arrows.
Off with you! Scat!
Ereshkigal calls.

Departure

From the great heaven she set her mind on the great below.
~ The Electronic Text Corpus of Sumerian Literature

Inanna abandons her duties
to descend to the underworld
seeking her sister Ereshkigal,
Queen of the Nether Kingdom.
She gathers together the seven *me.*
Seven divine powers she gathers in her hands.
The turban for travelling open country sits upon her head.
She loops blue lapis beads around her neck,
triple strands fall softly to her breast.
Royal robe wrapped about her hips,
she daubs her eyes with black mascara
called *Let him come. Let him come.*
The pectoral named *Come, man, come!*
she binds across her breasts.
Golden bracelets tighten round her wrists,
golden sandals clasp her feet,
fist holds lapis rod and measuring line.
Goddess readies.
Hoofs thunder,
wheels rumble,
dust flies.

Alone she quests, no man nor god
knows how she goes or why…

Inanna's Last Resort

Holy Inanna said to Ninshubar:
"Come my faithful minister...,
my escort who speaks trustworthy words.
I am going to give you instructions..."
~ The Electronic Text Corpus of Sumerian Literature

I implored her to forgo
the hazardous descent,
this strange encounter
with a dubious dark sister.

She made me place the jeweled diadem
upon her forehead, drape azure beads
around her royal throat and strap
the golden breastplate, named to taunt all foes,
across her full round breasts.

Beautiful vulva swathed in regal robes of state,
strong wrists encased in gold,
she raised the lapis rod and strode
barefoot and unafraid
toward the dim drear Underworld.

The regalia proved her sovereign,
but any man who saw those hips
would know his Queen.

If she fails to return
I'll bang the drums of war
to sound my fury!
I'll hammer the ears of gods.
I trust them not, but I shall beg.
Inanna thinks old Enki
will save the Queen of Heaven.

I hate this waiting!
Pace rooftop to rooftop
dodging laundry and bedrolls,
remembering how Inanna
snatched me in the midst of battle
from mother's lifeless body, shook
the breath into me as if I were a kitten,
bound me tight beneath her golden armor
and surged once more into fierce fray…

She kept me close as I was growing,
fed me from her breast and plate
till I grew tall enough to serve,
scrub latrines, peel potatoes,
train with weapons;
learning her ways
like a green sprout
leaping from the ground.

I've seen a hundred battles since.
Watched her fight, fists flying,
golden bracelets blasting light.

Light! Her strongest strength!
Sister to our Sun, she knows its every nuance.
What business has Inanna with the dark?

I've always stood beside her –
priestess, warrior, handmaiden
keeper of secrets.

Inanna's last resort.

Neti, Guardian of the Gates

"Let the seven gates of the underworld be bolted.
Then let each door of the palace...be opened separately."
~ The Electronic Text Corpus of Sumerian Literature

See these mighty pylons? I helped the masons
smooth that slip, incised Ereshkigal's beloved name
deep into clay, supervised each stroke and cut,
made sure each scribe cleaned and honed his stylus.

You think I've always worn fine linen?

I was once a shepherd boy run afoul of wolves.
Bleeding, septic, wandering in circles,
I stumbled on a heap of rags,
grabbed them up to staunch my wound
and found a babe, half-dead like me.
We made it to these very gates
before I died, becoming shade forever
in service to my queen.

Ereshkigal, who grew to rule this netherland,
raised me through the ranks – musician, scribe,
priest – till I became Chief Doorman of the Underworld
deciding who may pass and when. See my regulations
written all around the gate? The hours shades may gather,
when portals close and open; the rules of decorum?

Inanna flouted all. Her banging echoed through our halls,
rattling bedposts in my queen's most private chamber.

Orders came concise and clear.
"Close and lock the seven gates.
Let her pass them one by one,
but take one thing she carries hostage.
Then let the threshold open."

I bowed and ran.
Those days her wrath was like a tinderbox,
one spark might blow us all to smithereens.
She walked the endless corridors
for miles, endlessly wailing,
pregnant belly wrapped in mourning veils.
We feared her babe would die.
If nothing else, for bad or good, Inanna's advent
meant something shifted, something changed…

The goddess waited where I'd left her,
outside the gate at midday in full sun,
clad in armor forged of bronze.
Sweat gushed from underneath her turban,
dripped from nose to chin, pooled around her feet.
I never thought she would accept our terms,
but in she strode, brash, arrogant and glorious.
Even in death, her presence lingered like an aura
and in the end, she proved our savior.

Entering the Underworld

She put a turban,
headgear for the open country,
on her head.
~ The Electronic Text Corpus of Sumerian Literature

My sister's jealousy is not unfounded.
She is more beautiful, it's true,
but does not gleam as if some Midas
blew an errant kiss her way; her face
does not shine out upon the world
bright as burnished shields
reflecting in its lineaments
grief, joy, pain or rage
as if it were her own. No one
will scrutinize her shuttered face
or find reflection in her eyes.

I eat the adoration of the crowd,
drink every cup down to its bitter dregs,
alleviate suffering, enhance delight,
dine on a thousand and one stories –
Kishar's brutal husband, Anu's
tormented childhood, everybody's
mother. I listen well.

In return they sacrifice. Pour blood,
honey, milk and wine upon my altars.
Send song and incense mounting
heavenward in lazy rounds
to echo vultures' flight.

No wonder Ereshkigal is jealous.
No wonder she wanders caves
and sighs her way through tunnels.
Poor little burrowing owl
hiding in the dark.

Lately, I miss her.
I cannot say why.

Perhaps nobody else
can comprehend *my* story,
hear me tell the tales of battles won,
nights spent lustfully,
the spirit paths I wander
in convoluted dreams.

Neti, who guards the gate to hell,
asks me for my headdress,
a costly price to cross this simple threshold.

Christine Irving

Unwillingly I pay…

All clamors cease.

No whispered pleas, no shouted claims
for redress, recompense, reward.
No cheers, no praising adulation.
No voice except my own,
no thoughts but mine.

The door clangs shut behind me.
No way down, but down.

The Necklace of Blue Beads

She hung small lapis-lazuli beads around her neck.
~The Electronic Text Corpus of Sumerian Literature

Night and day, I wear a necklace of blue beads.
Mother strung the first on golden links,
placed it round my new-born neck.
Each birthday some new messenger appears
to add another azure orb.

A jackdaw drops the bauble in my lap,
a sky-blue pebble lodges in my shoe.
Texture varies, value too. Sapphire follows
last year's agate. Once, I find a blueberry,
dried, lacquered, drilled,
crowning my morning porridge.

Each dawn, I loop the beads three times,
my fingers know each contour.
Slipped through a fist, they tell the hours,
ease anxiety, quell tears,
prompt vision, underline
the sad epiphanies of hindsight.

Now an upstart gate guard
demands this precious necklace,
the blue mnemonic of my life
for passage through his portal.

Christine Irving

Though goddess of my own domain,
I cannot force my sister's gates.
The choice is clear – stay as I am?
Or gamble on some undetermined prize
Ereshkigal's bleak realm may offer?

This gateway is cerulean in color, hand-carved
from lapis stone. An omen? Who can say?
My jewels will hang above its threshold,
no hand but mine to touch them. Who cares
how sly the gate guard smiles behind his palm?
I will return to claim my own.

Something stirs beyond the shadowed gate.
Two watching cobalt eyes blink shut.
Dark prevails.

Birthright

She placed twin egg-shaped beads on her breast.
~ The Electronic Text Corpus of Sumerian Literature

I have worn them all my life,
twin egg-shaped trinkets dangling from my ears,
pinned to my chest or threaded on gold wire
embracing each round wrist.
They came into this world with me,
tiny fingers clenched around each bead.

My handmaids will not touch them, believe
their arcane inlaid patterns spell enchantment.
It's true they capture every errant ray of light, send
unexpected stabs of color darting toward the throne,
forcing Father's scowl, damping down
whatever joy my mother finds in me.

My people fear the power of double births; believe
they bring ill-luck – dark miasmas seeping
from twin skins to taint their air. I had a sister once.
They think I don't remember, but how should I forget
soft new limbs entangled with my own, our echoing hearts
the counterpoint to Mother's strong and steady pulse?

These trinkets told your fate, lost sister –
marked me as one to keep, left you exposed
forlorn upon the mountain top. Who found you?
Carried you beneath the ground? Have you ever
seen the sun, source of all illumination, glory
of our existence, whose name we utter as we pray?
How pale you must be, skin luminescent as the moon,
eyes grown wide as owls'.

Your creature stands before me now, dear twin.
His name Neti means, *to serve the gods*. I am god,
yet here I wield no power, cannot pass
without extending payment.

He wants the jewels clasped within my fists
as we were born. Taboo forbids,
on pain of death, I lose these talismans,
but eagerly I place the beads
upon his outstretched palm,
bend my royal neck, pass on.

The Power of Seduction

She pulled the pectoral which is called
"Come man, come," over her breast.
~ The Electronic Text Corpus of Sumerian Literature

This jeweled breastplate sees it share of gore.
It loves a war, singing, *Come man! Come!*
to call our enemies. Though honestly,
when bloodlust dominates
we take on any comers, foe or friend.
Unreason rules and only slaughter
slakes our thirst.

It takes beloved Ninshubar a week
to scrub each jeweled facet clean,
but when the armor shines again
it gleams so brightly on my chest,
floats so lightly, molding each round breast,
men groan to see me pass, and when
we whisper, honey sweet,
Come man! Come!
They do.

A most precious artifact, you would agree.
I take some time before I let it go.
But am I not Inanna? Goddess of War,
Lady of High Places, Queen of Love
and all Life's burgeoning fertility? What need
have I of tricks or sorcery to bring a man to bed
or slay a soldier? Breast adorned or bare
it's all the same to me. I let my armor go,
triumphantly!

Relinquishing the Ring

She placed a golden ring on her hand.
~ The Electronic Text Corpus of Sumerian Literature

My golden ring sends sparks into the dark.
Turn it deosil and even stone will burn.
Spin widdershins, extinguish any fire.
The power to pile up glowing charcoals
wraps my little finger. My hands
have mastered every craft –
the craft of the carpenter,
the craft of the coppersmith,
the craft of the scribe,
the craft of the leatherworker,
the craft of the fuller,
the craft of the builder,
the craft of the reed-worker.

But it wasn't always so.
Once, I walked alone, naïve, a maiden.
With my own light, I dazzled my father's eyes.
With my own mind' I engaged his intellect.
With my own guile, I tricked his powers from him
and gained them as my own. My charm
deflected anger, turned his wrath away.

What need have I
of golden rings to make my way?
Look how my eyes shine.
Look how my toes rest lightly on the ground.
I do not fear your dark.

Here! Take the ring and guard it well.
Warn Ereshkigal she wears it at her peril.
Gods are always seeking immolations.
I am no exception.

The Penultimate Gate

She held the lapis measuring rod
and measuring line in her hand.
~ The Electronic Text Corpus of Sumerian Literature

Approaching Ereshkigal's dark palace,
I must surrender lapis rod and line –
tools which measure space and time,
that plot the course of stars and sun,
of time triumphant – cities ground to dust,
crumbled cenotaphs, forgotten heroes.

Or time defeated – chiseled stone
year by year outlasting architects and builders,
earthquake, flood and empire's dissolution.
Ultimately futile, beautiful in daring and defiance,
my tools draw a line in sand to stand
against the force of circumstance and change.

Herein lies the power of gods to shepherd
nascent civil nations' birth, growth,
death and resurrection; bestow the gifts
that bless and curse agile primate minds
quickened with my own unquantifiable
ability to reason.

Christine Irving

I am Inanna, replete with other powers –
choice beyond choice surpassing computation.
Other gods may keep their paltry measures.
Done with definition,
I display two empty hands,
bend my back to stoop
beneath the lintel of this sixth
penultimate gate.

Beneath the Blood-Red Wall a Tunnel Opens

She covered her body with a pala dress,
the garment of ladyship.
~ The Electronic Text Corpus of Sumerian Literature

No guardian here to prod and prompt.
No direction needed, way lies clear,
message plain as dirt.

I shed my sequined gown,
rich with gold embroidery,
symbolic of my crown.

I am the Queen of Soil,
Harbinger of Spring, Seed Bearer.
Digging arm-deep, I turn compost
into humus. The liquors of my body
drip on Earth's detritus
converting it to loam.

Faced with this small portal,
I remember the rut of stag on doe,
how she stoops beneath his weight,
and bend my knees to graze full breasts
against the ground, wriggle hips
along the fertile earth.

My lust is vast enough
to spill through cosmic space,
fecund enough to conjure stars from dust,
it revels in humility.

Released at last
from every sensibility,
unbound, set free,
my climax shakes
Ereshkigal's dark throne.
Far far away in distant Ur
they feel Inanna's temples tremble.

Encounter

Then she made her sister Ereshkigal rise from her throne,
and instead she sat on her throne.
~ The Electronic Text Corpus of Sumerian Literature

Ereshkigal sits draped in heavy mourning.
Bloody nails that savaged sunken cheeks
now grasp a silver bowl of tears.
Rosy Inanna bereft of majesty and might
glows pink with satisfied desire.
Her hips swing wide with undiminished pride.
She does not bend her neck or bow.

Dark queen extends the basin.
Sister drink my tears.
Inanna turns her face aside.
Dark Queen leans forward,
offering one ravaged cheek.
Sister lick my wounds.
Inanna shakes her head from side to side.
Dark queen rises. *Sister take my seat.*

Inanna plumps a round warm bottom
down upon the black ice throne,
looks up to find Ereshkigal replaced.

Seven judges robed in phosphorescence
point toward Inanna, shout their sentence –
Guilty!

Death, they say and file away.

Gods cannot die, is her reply.

The words spin out into an empty hall,
losing momentum with every revolution.
Servants come and servants go,
polishing the throne room, cleaning, tidying,
hanging an abandoned corpse
neatly on a hook.

Seven Judges, Called Anuna

They spoke to her — it was the speech of anger.
They shouted at her - it was the shout of heavy guilt.
~ The Electronic Text Corpus of Sumerian Literature

We are the ones who see it all,
the ones who hear it all, who know
what really happened.
We remember everything.

We are the ones who weigh your heart.
We are the scales on which your heart
is weighed. We are the feather
by which your heart is measured.

If you travel underworld, beware.
Death lives in this domain.
We do not seek, but you may find us.
If you do, you'll know you died.

Re-birth is not within our jurisdiction.
For that you'll need a midwife.

Ninshubar Seeking Enki

> *"Father Enki, don't let anyone*
> *kill your daughter in the underworld."*
> ~ The Electronic Text Corpus of Sumerian Literature

It galls me to be running to some god for help.
I've importuned on bended knee
in sacred groves and sanctuaries,
sacrificed a dozen hens and pigeons.
There's only one place left to look.

It takes three days to find
Old Enki's rat-trap temple.
A fug of stale frankincense
and smoldering fruit
rolls down crumbling stairs
obscuring the uneven risers,
steep steps precarious
and wobbly. I hear
his bubbling water pipe
long before I reach him
lurking like a dragon,
atop his lofty ziggurat.

Propped listlessly upon a shabby silk settee,
he barely listens to my plea, but finally,
to stop my gad-fly voice,
scrapes the dirt beneath his nails
into one palm and spits,
stirs it with a finger,
conjures up two tiny
misbegotten entities with wings.

He whispers long into their ears,
then tosses them aloft. *Go!* he bellows.

I run away, but sneak back after midnight,
retrace the steep ascent to leave
a jug of ale upon his stoop.

Pray his creatures bring Inanna back.

A Troublesome Daughter

"What has my daughter done?
She has me worried. What has Inanna done?"
~ The Electronic Text Corpus of Sumerian Literature

She is troublesome – willful,
capricious, pitiless and clever,
all one could hope for in a god of war
(though not perhaps a daughter).
But goddess of love?
No love lost from that bosom,
although she prizes loyalty
above all else, rewards devotion well.
(It passes for affection.)

Ah, Inanna, sensuous and shameless,
she who brings bold men panting to their knees.
If you had seen her maiden state
with lust still burgeoning and unexpressed,
with sweet wine beaded on her nether lip,
pomegranate breasts set firm and round
beneath transparent linen, you would understand
how neatly she tricked me, took my seven powers,
won back forgiveness after breaking trust.

Oh, my daughter,
I treasure her ferocity.
I treasure her wild nature.
I treasure her pitiless glare.
I treasure her guile.
She is my darling, precious
beyond silver, gold and copper,
beyond lapis lazuli, more valued
than boxwood or cedar.

I will not let her metal be alloyed.
I will not suffer her split by the mason's stone.
I will not allow the carpenter to chop her.

The underworld shall not have her.
I will use the wits I gave her
to bring Inanna home.

Enki's Gala

He removed some dirt from the tip of his fingernail
and created the kur-jara. He removed some dirt
from the tip of his other fingernail
and created the gala-tura.
~ The Electronic Text Corpus of Sumerian Literature

We are *gala*,
Enki's hallowed creatures
formed from dirt.

Look how we fly, how we soar!
We who were lowest of low
made messengers of the gods,
born in service to Inanna,
beloved daughter of Enki, Lord of Earth,
Lord of Subterranean Waters.
He Who Is Wise Beyond All Others.
He Who Hears the Cries of the World.
He Who Answers with Compassion.
To us he entrusts the Water of Life.
To us he entrusts the Life-Giving Plant.

We dart past old Neti, gatekeeper
of the seven portals, slip silently
past creaking pivots, flit
like phantoms through his doors.

Ereshkigal's sad howl guides us.
Her grieving tears leak salt into the air.
We taste it on our lips, our own eyes weep
in sympathy. Her labor is upon her,
but avails nothing. Sorrow blocks her womb,
wraps its cord around the infant's throat.

Dead the husband who could comfort,
Heaven's mighty Bull has faded from the stars.
Absent the midwife to ease her travail.
The Anuna, maddened by her grief,
let no one near. She wails alone.

We cry beside her.
When she says, "Oh my heart,"
we say, "Oh your heart."
When she says, "Oh my liver,"
we say, "Oh your liver."

We hear her trouble.
We witness her pain.
She is seen. She is heard.
Her travail holds our attention.

Ereshkigal quiets.
Muscles loosen, fists unclamp.
Our solace surrounds her.
Babe turns, head down
within the womb.

In gratitude she offers rivers
and fields of ripened grain.
We beg Inanna's corpse.

The judges bring us putrid flesh.
Maggots crawl from every orifice,
blue veins like spider webs
trace livid skeins across her skin.

We wash her body in the Water of Life.
We place the Life-Giving Plant upon her tongue.
Enki's love shines forth, conquering death,
breaking taboo to reinstate his daughter.

We are *gala*,
Enki's hallowed creatures
formed from dirt.
We are the ones who witness,
the ones who will not
turn our eyes away.

Damuzi's Rant

Beat the drum for me in the sanctuary...
Lacerate your eyes for me, lacerate your nose for me.
In private, lacerate your buttocks for me.
~ The Electronic Text Corpus of Sumerian Literature

Inanna's gone it seems.
Ninshubar wants me to mourn, but even
at the worst of times I'm not a fan
of lacerating lamentations.
I prefer *my* cheeks intact.
Why disfigure precious flesh
this goddess loves so well?

Whatever happens, she will rage.
It is her nature, I'll keep my silken robes.
Let Ninshubar run begging, wrapped
in ragged toweling place to palace,
importuning gods to save her mistress.

I am the sacrificial ram, a creature of destiny
entangled in a tragic snare of predetermined fate.
The king must die, and I refuse to gamble
against a future preordained. I'd rather
seize the pleasures of this day – spiced wine,
a dish of honeyed plums and no insatiable Inanna
demanding to be tupped.

Restoration

Who has ever ascended from the underworld,
has ascended unscathed from the underworld?
~ The Electronic Text Corpus of Sumerian Literature

Body of clay.
Body of dirt.
Body of mud.
Covered in slime I come,
reborn into this world,
humbled.

How swiftly I departed life,
blew out and ceased to be.
Every mortal leaves a shadow,
but not Inanna, I left
no shade to wander ebon halls
and haunt a sister's dreams.

I return where I belong – to light,
traverse the seven gates
gathering my powers as I go.

My people need me.
I now know
that I need them.

What does it mean to change?

Body of clay.
Body of dirt.
Body of mud.
Covered in slime I come,
reborn into this world,
humbled.

Opening the Throat

And thus Inanna arose.
~ The Electronic Text Corpus of Sumerian Literature

Who-I-Am-Now arises singing!
From the silence of no sound
a wordless sound pours forth.
From the place of no sound
I make my first sound.

It has no meaning.
It has no context. Fresh-minted
as the newborn sun I rise to meet,
it sparkles with potential.

I will stamp it with the seal of my soul,
imprint upon it this new visage.
I will keep this sound, this not-yet word,
this guttural first utterance.

When future subtle complications
spin convoluted webs to fog my brain
I will call upon this new-knit body,
this constant resurrection,
to remember the noise I make today.

"Ughhhh," I will grunt, "Ughhh,"
as if I were in labor,
straining to give birth.

Who-I-Am-Now arises singing!
From the silence of no sound
a wordless song pours forth.

She Will Reward Me Royally

*"Cara is my singer, my manicurist and my hairdresser.
How could I turn him over to you? Let us go on."*
~ The Electronic Text Corpus of Sumerian Literature

Inanna comes like a bride from the desert,
from the west, the palace of death
she comes blazing. Alive! Splendid, terrible,
attended by demons.

Terror rolls me belly-up in dust,
but I cannot refrain searching
her bright countenance
for any flaw my art might modify.

Long tresses, midnight black, float upon
the wind of her coming. My sight
goes green with jealousy till I remember
hair grows on inside the grave,
remaining vital in the midst of death.

Did I not think my Lady dead?
Why else sit in dirt, garments rent,
eyes sore from salty tears?

Eager to fulfill their task,
snarling ghouls snark, growl, grab,
rip my tattered robe with filthy hands.
But, Inanna, seeing how I mourned,
moves them on to seek a substitute.

She will reward me royally.
I will trim and shape,
shampoo, set, plait and curry,
pretend I do not notice she is changed,
become less arrogant, more whole,
some empty place inside the heart
that cried to me, more full…

Utu, Sun God of Sumer

"Utu...my brother-in-law...Turn my hands...and...feet
into snake's feet, so I can escape my demons."
~ The Electronic Text Corpus of Sumerian Literature

I owe Damuzi, is all that I can say.
Men incur such debts from time to time.
Usually some small stupidity
gone catastrophically awry
fucks up your life in ways
more terrible than you could dream.
If in that moment, some brother
stoops to save you, one day
you'll be the answer to his prayer.

Still, I hesitate. My sister's wrath
can veil the sun in shadow,
send a pall across the Earth that makes
men writhe in terror on the ground
and cattle drop new calves before their time.

Inanna's rarely known to forgive,
but this time blood's not thick enough
to cancel obligation. Besides,
I drank Damuzi's milk. I ate his butter.

I turn his arms to serpent's coils,
his skin to slimy scale. He slips
the demons' grasp and flees, cohabitates
with some old woman and her son
inside a mangy sheepfold far away.

Inanna's been surprisingly forgiving.
Hymns to sunlight never go forgotten,
she tends my altar in her temple,
burns sweet incense, chants my names.

She's plotting plans, I know it,
hunkering on midden heaps
consulting with the Lord of Flies.
Damuzi will not taste sweet freedom long.

Half the Year

> *"You (Damuzi) half the year*
> *and your sister half the year…"*
> ~ The Electronic Text Corpus of Sumerian Literature

He was always golden,
best beloved recipient
of the biggest piece of pie –
smarter, quicker, more handsome
than any other boy.

Mama loved him best, last, foremost,
and I adored my brother. I followed him
everywhere, copied everything he did.
He called me "Sista-G", taught me to pee
standing up. Even now, when Mama's scolding
frays on my last nerve, I sneak behind
the sheepfold to pretend that I am
five years old again and artless.

It's hard being a girl, so many things to learn
that fill the days with chores. If you knew
how sick I am of spindles! They might as well
be shackles. I envy him. What would a day
completely free from feeding, lugging water,
washing, tilling, tending fire, be like?
I know it sounds insane to take his place
half-time beneath the ground, but this is all
I've ever wanted – to take his place.

My mother is ecstatic. Between wailing
for Damuzi she drops a word of praise,
the first I ever heard. Inanna is *most* pleased,
she hides it well, but I can tell – justice served,
vengeance taken, lover restored
and all because of humble Geshtinanna.
She owes me.

I hear Ereshkigal still mourns her mate,
perhaps she'll take sweet comfort in my company.
To please two queens, is no small thing.

PART II
Channeled

Channel: To enter a light trance in which the conscious and sub-conscious mind open more readily to one another allowing the imagination access to a deeper, more intuitive and empathetic kind of wisdom.

Workshop Poster

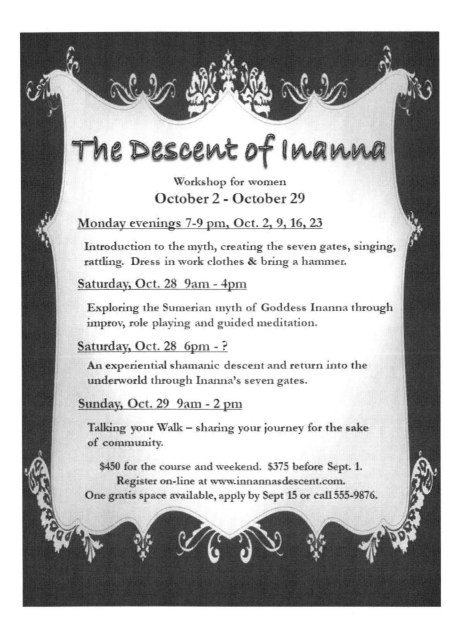

The Descent of Inanna

Workshop for women
October 2 - October 29

Monday evenings 7-9 pm, Oct. 2, 9, 16, 23

Introduction to the myth, creating the seven gates, singing, rattling. Dress in work clothes & bring a hammer.

Saturday, Oct. 28 9am - 4pm

Exploring the Sumerian myth of Goddess Inanna through improv, role playing and guided meditation.

Saturday, Oct. 28 6pm - ?

An experiential shamanic descent and return into the underworld through Inanna's seven gates.

Sunday, Oct. 29 9am - 2 pm

Talking your Walk – sharing your journey for the sake of community.

$450 for the course and weekend. $375 before Sept. 1.
Register on-line at www.innannasdescent.com.
One gratis space available, apply by Sept 15 or call 555-9876.

Preparation

Readying entails nine weeks of meeting. We study, pray, hammer, paste and paint. We cull from the storehouses of the Goddess – Dollar Stores, donations, dumpsters, attics, basements and stuff stacked free beside the sidewalk. Slowly we construct our seven gates.

Like a god who creates life from dirt beneath his nails, we transform our culture's bleak detritus into a whirling, swirling carnival of color – red, orange, yellow, green, sky blue, indigo, violet – rainbow color, chakra colors, atavistic colors – rendered meaningful within the magic cauldron of a woman's soul.

All day long, preparing for the journey, we tell Inanna's tales, sing her songs, dance to drums and beat our tambourines. Women channel voices from the mythic past – goddesses, gatekeeper, handmaiden, lover, take their places on our stage and strut soliloquies...

The Goddess Inanna: Channeled by Anh Johnson

Golden Utu, radiant brother Sun,
god of the cedar mountain,
I've gazed too long upon your dazzling aura
till every purple, blue, green, yellow, red
bleaches, bleeds and flees, leaving behind
only pallid corpses lacking definition.

How I long for shadow,
crave the comfort of caves –
labyrinthine passageways,
deep underground,
where my sable sister wanders
blind to baubles,
dumb to pleading praise,
deaf to envious adulation,
all the hurly-burly machinations
of those who lust for power.

I shall go to her
begging shelter,
seeking seclusion,
mustering courage
to scry in her dark mirror.

Ninshubar the Handmaiden:
Channeled by Michelle Jones

I am Ninshubar, the creaking pivot
round which the gate hinge turns.
Without me, the story stops.

I am she who importunes the gods,
plagues, annoys, persists,
cuts her losses, tries again.

Faithful watchdog, stubborn friend,
fighting beyond death,
never giving up.

Neti the Gatekeeper:
Channeled by Amanda Gilbert

She knocks aggressively upon our doors
demanding entrance, garbed in arrogance
bright as sunshine glancing off bronze armor,
jewels fine, fine, strung on gold,
and radiant raiment so unlike the dismal mourning
swaddling her sister's swollen belly
I cannot quell my indignation.

Ereshkigal was eldest! Born first, less blessed,
not quite as clever, strong or notable
and never one to laugh, unlike Inanna
who gurgled when a sunbeam kissed her,
never cried of hunger, cold or pain. Still,

she can love, whereas Inanna? Who can tell?
My mistress knows the name of every guard,
the herbs his mother grows in kitchen pots,
his father's recipe for beer.

She knows the moment gout attacks my toes,
sends me cherries from her trees, never
says a word, just pats my arm and slows
her step to match my crippled gait.

Married to the Bull of Heaven, she survived
thrived, learned his ways; teaching him
in slow degrees to love and be loved back.
His death has left her inconsolable.

Inanna ought to turn before it gets too late.
She is second born, usurper of the Dark Queen's
rightful place, complicit in the Great Bull's death.
Ereshkigal has yet to let her fury slip its bonds.

The Goddess Ereshkigal:
Channeled by Natalia Korsky

They try to comfort me with apples,
religion, philosophy, hot tea and platitudes
when all I want is lamentation; someone
to hear my cries and wail them back,
capturing each shriek and sob,
repeating them in symphony.

I need to know my anguish
impacts matter, leaves a dent,
a scratch across infinity's blank face.

Your sympathy's misplaced
your understanding useless.
I am drowned, engulfed,
swallowed by loss.
An echo to my grief
is all the lifeline you can offer.

Damuzi the Lover:
Channeled by Maria Costa

I know you women do not like me,
but who among you, if
I turned my gaze your way,
would long resist my liquid eyes,
my curling beard?

The very timbre of my voice sends
shivers down your spines
and deep inside yourselves you know
why women stay with men like me
and sisters sacrifice themselves for brothers
who never offer recompense
for wasted wealth or youth ill-spent
in undeserved devotion.

Inanna will forgive me.
She's done as much before.
I doubt she'll let the demons take
what she so ardently desires.

Even if she turns, the sun god owes me.
Utu's radiance reaches every corner,
illuminates or shadows, depending on his whim.
He'll ferret out a hidey-hole. You'll see.

The Goddess Inanna:
Channeled by Sarafina Crosby

In the dark Ereshkigal awaits me,
ebony sister hiding from the light.
Jealousy gnaws at her bones. She hates me.
Pushed deep into my dungeon, out of sight
she is my twin, my Siamese adjunct.
The cords are stretched that bound us once like one,
but never broken, cut, ripped out, defunct,
just buried deep, all memory outrun
avoiding agony to no avail
for finally, I cannot stop despair.
It seeps through every crack until her jail
becomes my own, her pain my own to bear.

If happiness is what you seek to find
unearth the dark, free all you've left behind.

Inanna's journey illustrates a profound psychological truth – to mature in life the ego must periodically die and re-create itself in closer alignment to that elusive quality called authenticity.

The women pictured in the following poems create a ritual to enable change by releasing a belief, assumption or dream that no longer serves them. This letting go creates an empty space into which something new, something more serviceable may flow.

The commonality of their endeavor provides comfort and courage, while the structured confines of ritual space create a safety zone in which deep and often terrifying psychological work can be done without dogma, obligation or expectation. Participating in ritual, they serve both themselves and each other.

Christine Irving

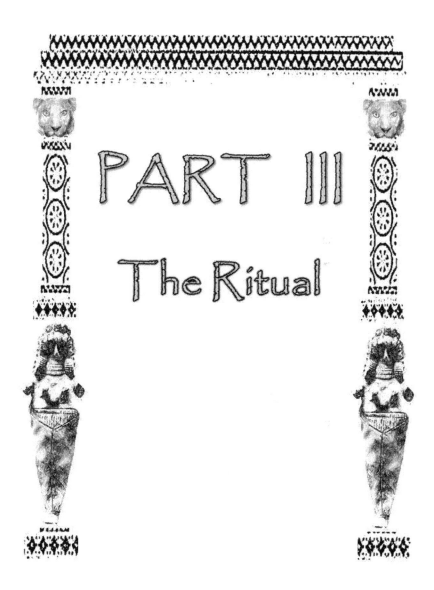

PART III

The Ritual

73

The Journey

The room lies quiet, windows flung wide open; a silver bowl of water set upon the sill. Ebony cabochons and moonstones, cuttings of rosemary and mugwort, welcome in the night. Seven gaudy gates, turned beautiful by starlight, spiral round the room curling inward like a chambered nautilus to still dark center. Poet-priestess Enheduanna's words, written 5,000 years ago, sung this very afternoon by living women, have filled this space with presence so palpable it seems to breathe...

After feasting on goat cheese, bread and honey, after ritual baths infused with peppermint, wormwood and lavender, dressed in jewels and robes, women journey through seven gates; disrobing as they go, to crawl at last, naked and alone, into the black tomb/womb constructed at the spiral's center. Emerging like butterflies sprung from chrysalides, they cross the seven thresholds to ascend once more into this world. Finally, enjoined to silence till they meet again, the women sleep.

By morning the gates are gone; room cleansed and rearranged around an armchair adorned with seven gauzy veils. One by one each woman takes the throne to tell the tale of her passage — what was lost, regained; what found or let go. They do not travel for themselves alone, but also for their sisters. Every step resonates within some other heart; bright or shadowy reflections filling gaps, answering unasked questions...

This is the lesson of Enki's gala – healing begins by looking past the mirrored shields of self, to see, hear, touch and smell each other; to grok through instinct and experience the distilled essence of some other soul...

Come! Listen to their telling...

Gathering

Maiden to matriarch, we gather
drawn together by our oldest recorded tale –
life, death, rebirth,
the Descent of Inanna,
Sumerian goddess of old.

Hearsay, gossip, word of mouth,
timeworn sources, comforting
to women, more true than men imagine,
call us to this autumn rite.

Invoking the goddess,
women shout *Inanna!*
to the stars. We take our places.
This ritual may last till dawn.

We'll traverse seven thresholds,
disrobing gate by gate
to die symbolically and then
replace, retrace, reclaim;
re-member our lost selves
with what the dark returns.

Shared tales searing as acid,
mild as milk, will spill from every orifice
onto the all-forgiving ground.

You might suppose
we come back clean as babes,
purged and lightened, but secrets
do not vanish. Once brought to light,
beyond mere coping, every revelation
demands its due.

What once lived far below
in moon-bereft darkness
will now require tending.

Maria Acosta:
Violet Gate, Descending

The man pursued persistently,
Learnt me like a poem
he must memorize or fail.

His knowledge served him well…
They call it 'brainwashing'
the forced scrubbing out of old beliefs

replacing everything I once held dear
with dependency, self-doubt, and fear.
On our honeymoon, I never slept.

He woke me nightly, again
and again for soliloquies and sex.
It felt romantic.

He selected every bite I ate, handled
all money, chose each souvenir.
Once he'd carried me across his threshold

the beatings began.
I know it seems impossible
how quickly I succumbed…

Christine Irving

Random awakenings, shattered
dishes, incessant supervision, each day's
persistent petty humiliations…

Numbed into acquiescence
I waded dumbly through the years
until one afternoon, two women

gossiping in the grocery line
discussed their battered neighbor.
"Me," I thought, "That's me."

Now, here I am, untethered,
not yet free, but on the way.
The gatekeeper holds out her hand.

Stripped naked,
these wedding pearls are all I carry,
all I have to give.

Hers is the only threshold I will cross tonight.
Already I'm exhausted, but must try
to understand what came to be and why.

Must let some glimmer of forgiveness
light up the emptiness through which
my shattered spirit wanders.

Minnie Goodman:
Indigo Gate, Descending

Mama wanted a normal little girl.
Her smile turned upside down when I
two-stepped with the evening breeze,
led fireflies across a dusky lawn;
told her what the flowers whispered
while she tucked me into bed.

And I could find lost things!
Guess right, every time, what song
the radio would play. It scared her.
She thought some devil spirit
possessed my soul
and punished every fantasy –
lye soap on the tongue,
birch wand on the bottom,
bread and water in my room.

I closed my ears,
curbed my lying tongue,
kept eyes glued to ground.
Stopped dancing. Don't remember
any colors after five years old,
nothing from my childhood,
but Mama's scold…

Christine Irving

On my thirty-fifth birthday,
scanning a bulletin board
for weekend yard sales
one word blazed out – Inanna!
written in rainbow.

Now I sit in a circle on the floor
with women I don't know
draped in veils and costume jewels
from a rummage bin in the corner.

Someone's painted my whole face indigo
drawn a luminous third-eye, wide open,
in the middle of my forehead.

Sylvia Peabody:
Sky Blue Gate, Descending

I paint women who have lost their voices.

Tongues lie bleeding on the floor,
loll limp from over-stuffed designer handbags.
They follow their owners on leashes like little dogs
or act as bookmarks to hold a place in fairy tales
read by girls with bloody drops oozing from their lips.
Modeled after Kahlo, my self-portraits bear visible wounds,
throats pierced by empty holes where once a larynx lay.

The Voice Box Series is famous –
gilded words stuffed inside
small ornate cubes of Plexiglas
bound in silken ribbon,
silver wire and golden thread.

Last night, I bought a leather gag
in a sex shop round the corner,
stayed awake till dawn
stitching beads of semi-precious stones –
lapis, turquoise and blue topaz
outlined in silver sequins.

When I bind my mouth,
I want the ugly thing to blaze!
Reminding you how very many ways
exist for men to steal a woman's voice.

Cicely Johnson:
Green Gate, Descending

Two hearts
beat deep within my chest,
one inside the other, out of sync.

The inner one is like a turgid purple bruise,
blood swollen tight beneath a skin too small,
grown impervious with long denial.

This is where I ought to build an altar,
sacred sanctuary where Spirit mothers me,
fosters intimacy between disparate selves
estranged from one another.

Instead of treasuring my extra heart as holy ground,
I use it as a cubby-hole – storage space
for all that's mean or mingy,
dank and dim and stingy.

The other, larger heart beats pulpy soft,
too big, too red, bared willingly
for all the world to feast upon –
except for me and mine.

I spend my lifetime helping others,
every wound a siren call,
but never hear my family's cry
above the endless sound
of others' anguished hearts
or notice they are pushed aside
by all the homeless, lame and sick
suckling at my teats.

The cries of the world
sound right outside my window.
They will continue, ever after ever,
while from expanding distances
my children wave good-bye.

Sheila Malone:
Yellow Gate, Descending

I love the righteousness injustice offers.
Resistance make me bold, defines me.
Righteousness whitewashes all mistakes,
flaunts my certainty, denies all doubt.

Three marriages gone, countless jobs lost,
I own my own business - no staff, one
insanely faithful friend, a dog and road rage.

Forced by arbitration
to attend group therapy,
I can't ignore the tales of lives
lived parallel to mine – so different
in premise, so similar in suffering.

Their details slide beneath my thickened skin,
splinters of grief, courage, fear,
denial, and determination.

Change or die, a woman murmurs.

The room stills instantly.
Blood thumps along my veins,
vision blurs. I cannot catch my breath.
Can I forego rebellion?

A rebel yell rips out my throat.
I howl, cry, vomit on the carpet.
Women mop the mess.

Intention, start with intention…

Tonight, I'll focus on yellow,
color of YIELD, color of will.

What is the difference
between willingness and will-full?

I close my eyes, imagine myself,
entering a busy freeway without umbrage,
take the first baby-step
toward surrender.

Christine Irving

 Natalia Korsky:
Orange Gate, Descending

Coiled thoughts chase their tails,
rolls of film replayed and worn, scratched thin
with time, grooves dug so deep in neurons
a thousand years could not erase their tracks.

Can they be stopped without blunt force
or bullets to the brain? Tell me how
to unclench fist, unfurl palm, let go…

No, don't! In truth, I like this ride!
The loop-de-loops, the fearsome upward slog,
the awful rush toward madness;
even the down dull flats of despair
comfort me with intimate familiarity.

Why should I relinquish rush?
Abrogate addiction?

Carma Wong:
Red Gate, Descending

It's a stand-off. Me and my son,
defiant as two bull dogs.
He is four. I am forty-two.
Shoulders hunched, fists curled
he tucks his chin. Daddy's blue eyes
glare back at me.

I am prepared to laugh, not flinch.
Feel love, not violent rage
unexpected as a volcano
erupting in my placid plain.

My father's scowl
on the face of my little boy.

I am the volcano.

I want to shake him,
twist his arm, beat him
till his blood runs…

Welts break out along old scars,
circle my wrists,
crisscross my buttocks,
trail down my thighs.

The child trembles.

I turn on my heel,
run for our lives,
lock the bedroom door,
slide the key beneath it.

"Take it, hide it, call your Dad."

My dust-free, calm,
well-ordered room
enfolds me like a blanket.
I suck my thumb and rock.

Did I run away,
change my name,
my hair, my act, marry
a kind and gentle man,
paint the nursery blue –
all to raise a monster
like the monster who raised me?

It's why I must
descend down into darkness.
Forgetting didn't work,
denial failed...
I will not kill myself
nor beat my son.

Ishtar Gate Lion
Pergamon Museum Berlin

Interlude

One by one as women find their places, I the guardian dim the lights. Now only one candle burns, beside a pile of cushions.

We need a guardian in case of meltdown. A look into the mirror of one's self can overwhelm. Faced with hidden truths suddenly revealed, even the wisest women falter. Something unexpected always comes, no matter how prepared we think we are – a childhood slight, so light its trace is barely visible; some incidental feature in another person's story. You never know. Our minds are infinite storehouses; every memory, every feeling recorded somewhere, subject to retrieval.

A woman naps among the cushions, snoring softly, steadily, like a little drumbeat, creating a rhythm, setting the pace. This work's exhausting. That's why I've gathered water, chocolate, almonds, aspirin, Kleenex, essence of lavender, geranium and bergamot. From time to time a woman comes to hold my hand and whisper or lay her head upon my lap and cry. I don't reply, just listen, squeeze her fingers, stroke her hair, anoint her with my oils.

At nine, I'll ring the gong; swing my little hammer seven times against the cymbal, pausing between hits to let the echoes play.

This signals the ascent. Time to return. No matter how reluctantly they first began, most have learned at least one thing tonight – to love the dark. But now it's time to shoo them out, let them lave their hands and face or shower.

I'll burn some sage, clear whatever demons linger, let the room breathe quietly. I too will leave, change black robes to gold, become Inanna Rising and lead them back above the ground. The journey's but half over. The climb can be so steep...

Mercy, compassion, care, lenience and homage are yours, and to cause flood storm, to open hard ground and to turn darkness into light.

~Hymn to Inanna
The Electronic Text Corpus of Sumerian Literature

Sarafina Crosby:
Red Gate, Ascending

I wake in darkness
dreaming of storm shelters and tornadoes.
I don't know where my anger's gone –
my life line, the shield I carried like a trophy
through nine whole weeks, listening to women
whine about fear, wounds and suffering.

I'd kept silent, refused to share,
helped them build their kitschy gates.
Don't know why I stayed the course,
crossed each threshold to end up naked
in a pop-up, one-woman tent bereft of rage,
only thing I've ever called my own.

I fought so hard to stay alive, survive,
yet here in this symbolic tomb
the thought of dissolution comforts.
I'd lingered, to be last inside,
"No rush," they said, "no hurry,"
and I have nowhere else to go.

Certainly not up, into a world
that never wanted me, yet now…
something about emptiness
excites anticipation –
that empty spot, where fury dwelt,
begins to pulse and yearn.

I squirm like a full-term baby,
whose womb has grown too small.
Darkness contracts
to spit me out unready.
Whatever follows survival,
suddenly I crave it.

Michelle Jones:
Orange Gate, Ascending

I slept through my sojourn in the Underworld.
First time in months, I haven't cried myself to sleep.

Death is a dreary business. It sags
breasts, thins hair, cracks lips
till lipstick wicks into the tiny
new lines etched around my mouth.

They resemble little stitches,
like the monster's in a horror flick,
half-dead face basted awkwardly together.
I cannot stop lamenting,
re-telling the story endlessly,
though no one listens anymore.

This descent barely touches me.
I find the gates ridiculous
and whose idea was glitter?
It sheds. Grinds into the carpet,
scatters like demented dandruff
across everyone's shoulders.
It's not what I expected.
not the relief from misery
I'd hoped for, paid for…

Still, I could have slept forever
in their tent thingy – deliciously dark,
not a crack of light anywhere,
perfect refuge till a fly arrived
to buzz me out of black oblivion.

I almost bail during break time.
Hide inside a toilet stall
long after the last chime sounds,
emerge to find a Wailing Wall
built of cardboard packing boxes.

Women rock and cry,
scribble lamentations
across its dull facade.
Here it is at last!
The thing I came for.

I lean into the makeshift barricade,
press forehead to its surface.
Nothing else has the texture of cardboard,
feels like the sound fingernails make
scraping across chalkboard or the way
raw spinach squeaks along teeth.
It's an uncomfortable material,
appropriate for mourning.

Our howling fills the room –
screams, moans, groans,
every way we creatures
express our anguish,
share despair.

Christine Irving

Cacophony rises to crescendo,
voices meld in random requiem.
It soars from underneath our soles
through sex, gut, heart, out open throats
in one concerted wail of shared loss
so unexpectedly comforting
we quiet.

I rise and bend to kiss the head
of every woman sharing sorrow.
Free of grief's first inconsolable
hyperbole, I shoulder mourning,
begin to soldier on.

Tiffany Graves:
Yellow Gate, Ascending

I crouch in the shadows watching a gaggle
of middle-aged women wailing their hearts out
beside a stack of cardboard boxes pretending to be a wall.
At least they've put their clothes back on!
Can't believe my momma bobbing her bare boobs around.
Don't know what's got into her. Since she turned forty
seems like she took a spotlight off me,
aimed it somewhere I can't see, inside herself.

She caught me fair and square breaking her rules.
Made me choose – come or be grounded, but no way
I'm stripping down or crawling my naked butt
into some make-believe 'underworld!'

I wish she wouldn't cry. Never saw her cry before.
Heard her sometimes… late at night…
Afraid I run with a bad crowd, scared
I don't have any backbone. Faults herself
for acting too protective, too shielding.

Yellow lights looped along the lintel,
shine on raven hair and honey-satin skin.
Momma looks so lonely sitting there.
Shoulders bowed I used to ride so high on
fingers holding tight to braids we called my 'reins.'

Most all my life, she's worked two jobs
fought to keep me in crayons and coloring books,
bicycles and tennis shoes that twinkled. I used to think
her strength made me weaker, but that's not right,
just my excuse for doin' what I shouldn't.

Just can't bear to see her unsupported.
Move to sit behind her, spine-to-spine.
Hand inches around, takes hold of mine.
Her back feels solid, warm. I push in closer.

Heat rises from our tailbones, curls around
each vertebra, braiding us together the way
our DNA links us to our great, great, great,
great-grandmothers.

Momma's fingers tighten around mine.
She feels it too, feels us begin to glow
like lanterns and lightning bugs. Suddenly
I see through Momma's eyes!
Ramshackle gates shimmer
with magic and meaning, each woman
radiates in singular beauty.

My sight returns. Room's the same, gates
tacky as ever, but the ladies still shine like stars.
I turn, wrap arms and legs around my mother,
rest my chin upon her shoulder, accept
who she is, acknowledge my own accountability,
assume my own power.

Amanda Gilbert:
Green Gate, Ascending

Someone is searching for me.
I wear the sealed letter folded thin,
tucked beneath my bra's left cup
right above my sealed heart.

At ten my Uncle Dom seduced me.
At twelve I bore a child conceived
before my first menstruation.

You think you know my story,
but you don't. He was my only kindness,
saw me, knew me, taught me folks
have reasons for acting like they do.
Told me always search out why.

My mother was an addict drunk on Jesus.
Alcohol or drugs could not be worse.
Christ her phantom lover, her bliss, her all,
was a god who did not suffer children.

When I began to show
they sent me to a place up-state,
where grim-faced wardens schooled
unwed children in deprivation and discipline,
sealed us in silence, forbidding questions,
friends and conversation.

Never saw my child, don't know its sex.
Uncle Dom moved family elsewhere,
no forwarding address. Thanks to Mother's
clear directive, cold as a surgeon's scalpel,
I'll never bear another child.

The gatekeeper holds out her hand.

Shall I place the letter in her palm?
Let her break the seal? Or wonder
ever after, what might have been?

Lilly Parvase:
Sky Blue Gate, Ascending

I arrive in underworld like a hunted thing,
hair in tangles, mascara running down my cheeks,
battered as a beaten rug. Detritus of my past
shakes out, carried away by the spirit winds
blowing through these gates.

Darkness offers respite, solace, solitude,
but now it's time to leave. It's hard to go.
Scrambling out I bump someone.
Too dark to see. She bends to me,
whispers in my ear,
"I love your song."

What song?

Approaching the Red Gate
doorkeeper blocks my entrance.

"Tell me your deepest heart's desire."

I thought ascent would be easier.
Knowing what I want turns out to be
even more difficult than giving shit up.
I burst into tears. She steps aside.

Christine Irving

One by one I pass through portals –
red, orange, yellow, green,
query still unanswered.

Deep inside me
someone struggles to reply
and all the while that other question nags.

What song?

(I used to sing, till second grade choir
when Miss Barrymore made me lip sync
"My Country Tis of Thee" during assembly.)

The ubiquitous gate-guard
has strapped a paper beak across her nose,
stuck an aqua ostrich feather in her hair.

"Sing your song," she demands
What song?
"Sing your song."

Every voice I vanquished on the way down
flies back – all the woulds, coulds, shoulds,
can'ts, won'ts, don'ts besiege my brain.
Breath strangles in my throat, light dims.

The guardian transforms before my eyes
mask to flesh, flesh to feather.
Half-bird, half-woman, she stands beside me
one warm hand upon my diaphragm,
the other on my back, right behind my heart
as if she held it pulsing in her palm.

"Breathe," she whispers in my ear.

Her breath smells of raspberries and rain.
Soft as a lullaby she sings to the directions,
east, south, west and north,
asking for inspiration, courage,
insight and compassion to waft
through my lungs, infuse my blood
stiffen my spine, ground my feet…

And so it is.

"Start with your name. Sing your name."

It comes as a croak and a squeak,
slow trickle before the dam
begins to spurt and break.

THIS is what I want!
I want to sing!

I am singing.

Martha Sweetwater:
Indigo Gate, Ascending

Someone placed an armchair by this gatepost
and tossed a throw across the battered seat,
a celestial map picked out in gold on an indigo field
inviting me to sit and ponder darkness.

How do we define the underrated dark?
Element? State? Quality? Absence?
Mystery is the only word I find to fit,
yet it supplies no answers,
by definition - undefinable.

Two lids slide shut, third-eye wakens;
dark-adapted, quick to see patterns
weaving cosmic time and space
into spider web connections
between all matter born of stellar dust.

Old wounds and ancient suffering
take on new meaning, glide gently into context,
shrink in the face of expanding universes
and quantum microcosms. Intuition blossoms.

I sense the Guardian, the Watcher Within step forth.
She shelters orphan, fool and hero
beneath her wide-spread wings.

Dark feathers
brush my sleeping cheek in benediction,
waking me from my dreamtime vision.

This journey, moving upward toward the sun,
warms old bones, fills young eyes
with beauty unsurpassed.

I welcome light –
the way one greets a child –
relishing its joy in learning,
but treasure more
the blessed dark's great gift
of vast un-knowing.

Anh Johnson:
Violet Gate, Ascending

Artificial blooms, garlands of iris,
lavender, morning glory, violet
veil our first and final gate in flowers.

Real violets contain ionone,
a chemical component that switches
a nose's scent receptors on and off,
making the aroma of violet
alluring as illusion.

Whiffs of floral fragrance keep wafting by.
It reminds me of another journey, long ago…

Lotus blossoms and candles float downriver
riding to the sea beside leaky overcrowded boats,
aunties, uncles, cousins, mother –
escaping constant terror,
the incessant necessity to trust no one,
unrelenting inevitable change for the worse…

My mother wore my father's dog tags.
They are the price I paid to journey underworld.

Return to Inanna

American grandparents bought me from my mother.
They raised me white, half my lineage erased
by her kept promise never to return.

I spent a lifetime following
elusive scents of kindred, home, tribe,
country to country, until I found it
everywhere that women meet,
share stories, help each other fathom
the meaning of their lives.

Listening to their tales I see connections
interwoven like daisy chains
stretching back in time to First Mother.

Stars collide, dust coagulates to matter,
random lightning bolts awaken life.
A bat flaps wings and blows
the malarial mosquito it would have eaten
out to sea to bite a fisherman
who carries the disease back home
that kills his child.

Memories buried deeper than our histories
ride on the backs of fragrance and stench,
blurring boundaries between imagination
and experience.

Whiffs of floral fragrance continue wafting by.

Did someone scent these fabric flowers
or could it be a spectral visitation?
Gods and saints are known to emit
sweet odors and hanker after incense.

How infrequently facts define truth!
Reality folds back upon itself in pleated layers
overlaid like geological formations
adamantine in appearance, but plastic over time,
capable of movement however incremental.

I shan't reclaim those dog tags. No longer need
an unknown father's worn magic
to dispel my cherished chimeras –
severance and rejection.

Janis Joplin sang, "freedom's just another word
for nothin' left to lose" – a cynic's adage,
but it rings sweetly true to me.

Tonight, I leave my bitterness behind –
the whole array of would, should, could
if only this, or that, or the other thing
had not, did not, ought not to have happened…

I claim kinship with stardust,
study the efficacy of emptiness;
a willing subject, wherever I wander,
to the startling effects of butterfly wings.

Merry Meet Again

We come from the east, daughters of the dawn inspiring each other with stories of hardship overcome. We come from the south full of fire, impassioned sisters longing to awaken our true selves. We come from the west, learning from dreams the medicines we need with which to heal wounds. We come from the north full of grace and gratitude, sharing our wisdom with all who wish to know.

Cardinal spirits surround us. The spirits of above shower us with blessings. The spirits of below accompany us along the way. Here at journey's end, in the heart of home, we gather beneath Inanna's wings; hesitate to wander or disperse; linger for a last embrace, fingers tightly clasped in circle, to sing another round...

> *"The circle is open, but unbroken.*
> *May the love of the Goddess*
> *be ever in your heart.*
> *Merry meet and merry part*
> *and merry meet again..."* *

---

* https://www.youtube.com/watch?v=N-rWiFyAUnE

Enheduanna Freed

Stanza follows stanza,
epic journey of descent,
relinquishment, return,
death and putrefaction,
reconciled siblings,
grief and consolation,
rebirth…

Boots sound upon stone steps.
Keys jangle in a warden's hand.

Humbled, bathed, pardoned,
triumphant priestess
wends her fragrant way to temple.
Prostrates body. Stills
her singing mind.

Vision, sight, true seeing
gifted by the Goddess.

Window opening through time –

4,000 years of immortality,
every poet's dream.

The following section includes generic guidelines to creating a ritual, a Call to Directions specific to an Inanna-based ritual and an invocation to Inanna. Please feel free to copy and redistribute these three articles. They have my name and website printed on the bottom of the pages, I'd appreciate it if you would include them if you use these as handouts.

Blessed Be.

~Christine Irving, December 2018

PART IV

Creating Your Own Ritual

What Makes It Ritual?

A ritual is a co-creative act in which one consciously engages with the numinous to create a meaningful ceremony dedicated to a specific purpose. This collaboration between ourselves and whichever ineffable entity, with whom we maintain relationship, is what differentiates ritual from a workshop, event, entertainment or tradition. These other happenings may contain a spiritual element, but do not necessarily allow the ineffable place for innovation and spontaneity.

One of the hallmarks of ritual is that it arouses that pleasurable feeling of engagement, anticipation and excitement we associate with play. Like play, ritual is serious, participatory and fun. It engages us completely, uniting the human need for safety and familiarity with the need for novelty and risk. Ritual contains an implicit expectation of surprise.

The descent ritual depicted in *Return to Inanna* is based on a specific intention to release whatever drains ones inner power and reclaim that which may enhance it. Whatever ones motivation, ritual can be extraordinarily nourishing and healing, especially when approached humbly and in gratitude. Many kinds of reasons exist for creating and using ritual:

Lamentation – the sanctioned expression of grief, catharsis.

Commemoration – the retelling of creation stories, remembrance of origins, ancestors, the founding of the community, holiday celebrations, memorials, etc.

Celebration – communal acknowledgements of rites of passage – births, weddings, comings of age, birthdays, etc.

Stress Relief – Carnival, April Fool's Day, May Day, Sadie Hawkins Dance, etc.

Healing – the laying on of hands, prayer, shamanic work, planting and harvesting healing plants, mixing of healing salves and tonics, etc.

Spirituality – Religious ceremony, magic, exorcism, devotion, etc.

Ritual is a form of sacred theater purposefully designed to evoke our willingness to welcome the divine. You may treat it as the art form it is, using costumes, props, music and lighting to create an atmosphere that enhances your intention to invoke Presence.

All art is transitory and nothing is more transitory than theater; every play a one-night stand, each performance different; no matter how closely actors stay on-script. There's a saying that when man plans, God laughs. Do not expect your ritual to unfold exactly as you crafted. You are inviting the unknown to play with you on its own terms, and it will.

Remember traditions vary widely! In many ways the world is moving towards fusion. We see it in food, fashion, architecture and relationship – humankind's basic wants and needs (sustenance, clothing, shelter and social contact). Creatively mixing and matching to create a unique ritual of your own is perfectly appropriate.

However, if you intend to *re-create* a ritual indigenous to a particular culture, be very respectful. Consider carefully questions of cultural colonialism. Research to make sure you understand the significance of movements and symbols you will use in your re-creation. Ask permission of an elder, priest or shaman of the culture whose ritual you wish to use. If this should prove unfeasible, attempt to contact the ancestors by way of vision, sleeping dream or lucid dreaming and ask them for permission. If they say "no," abide by that decision without arguing or demanding explanation.

The next article in this section of the book, offers a basic formula to guide you in creating your own rituals. These are not rules, only time-honored cross-cultural techniques evolved from questions we humans have always asked ourselves. How do we connect to mysteries whose presence we sense, but cannot prove? How can we approach the mystery we both long for and fear, while remaining safe? What can we create, as a group, that will prove meaningful to all, while strengthening the bonds between us?

The unknown can be unpredictable. Be cautious in your asking. Share. Laugh. Set careful boundaries and clear intentions. Express gratitude. These guidelines are designed to take the edge off fear and keep everyone safe together.

Rituals create an empty space and offer it to Spirit. An empty space is a place of pure potential, inside which anything is possible. Once defined, it becomes an open doorway, a playground; a dance floor.

In my experience, if one leaves room enough for the unknown to appear, it always does. Something wonderful, greater than an individual or group, enters the circle and offers a moment's respite from self-defined ego and ordinary reality.

While designing your ritual, always keep this maxim in mind:
Whoever comes are the right people.
Whenever it happens is the right time.
Whatever happens is the right thing.
When it's over, it's over.

A Formula for Ritual

Women, children and men have always created ritual. It is the wellspring from which art, drama, music, poetry and dance arise. Although individual components may vary wildly, many rituals, whether they be ancient, modern, familiar or foreign, follow the same basic pattern:

I. Designation of Space

Ritual takes place in liminal space – a kind of no-man's land situated between different planes of reality; an imaginal place acting as a doorway between the known and the unknown. To create such a space, locate a setting that is as quiet and private as possible. Mark out a circular boundary, actually or symbolically, with stones, ribbons, branches, fires, incense, words, motions, etc. Sometimes people place a shrine or altar in the center or to one side of the circle or set an altar at each of the four cardinal points (east, south, west and north).

An altar is a table, an ancient sign of home and hospitality. It can be decorated and furnished or left empty depending on one's purpose; possibly to hold representational objects personal to the participants and/or significant to the ceremony.

II. The Gathering

Usually one enters the space ceremoniously. Sometimes people are symbolically cleansed with light, sound or smoke as they enter through a designated entrance to form a circle with their bodies. (A circle allows every participant to see the face of every other participant. If a campfire burned in the center of

www.christineirving.com

the circle, every member would receive an equal share of light and warmth.)

III. Calling the Directions

The contemporary ceremony of Calling the Directions comes to us through the teachings of Native Americans from many nations. However, this practice is common to almost all cultures and transcends tribal and national barriers as well as those of time and space. It may be one of humanity's oldest extant rituals. In Calling the Directions we humans acknowledge that we are NOT the center of the universe around which all else revolves. We recognize that bigger mysteries are present here with us, vaster than we can grasp or understand.

Again, there is no right way to do this. Many variations exist and it's completely appropriate to change the format to fit your theme or intent. This is the format I most often use:

While the directions are being addressed, each person turns with the herald(s), who face and call aloud to the East, South, West and North. (Some groups add the Above, Below and Center as directions.) The herald is a designated person or volunteer. Her/his address may include a description of the attributes associated with a particular direction. For example, East is often associated with air, dawn, insight, inspiration. Traditions vary *greatly* and you can create your own symbolism. The doing is more important than the how.

Directions are called in order to:
> 1) Orient ourselves in space and time and bring ourselves into full presence - grounded, conscious and willing to pay full attention.

2) To acknowledge and honor the local spirits and guardians of the land we stand on, ask their permission to continue and welcome their participation.

3) To give notice to the denizens of other realms that we intend to open a door between our worlds in order to undertake sacred work and to invite their participation and blessing.

IV. Invocation

A statement of intention addressed to a specific ancestor, mentor, spirit, deity or idea, which may include praise for the entity addressed and a plea for guidance in carrying out the intention.

V. The Work

A specific action undertaken by all the participants that furthers the stated intention, i.e. creating care packages, guided meditation, channeling, a skit, the laying on of hands, scrying, knitting warm socks for the homeless, etc. The possibilities are endless.

VI. Raising the Energy

Song, dance, drumming, toning, etc., in which all participate to intentionally move psychic and physical energy of both the group and individual from slower to faster, lower to higher until a crescendo is reached. At a given signal, everyone releases the energy they've raised into the atmosphere to go where it is needed.

VII. Closure

Any last-minute summation or instruction. (Sometimes it is hard to transition back to normal existence. A warning about driving carefully or taking time to process, might be in order.)

Thanking and bidding farewell to the directions. Herald(s) who called the direction in are usually the ones who bid it farewell. To close, reverse the order in which you started to call the directions. If you started facing East and ended facing Center, when closing, begin with the Center and end with the East.

Announcement or acknowledgement through traditional words or song that the ritual is over and the circle is open. (See page 110)

Creating Your Own
Inanna-based Ritual

Creating your own ritual of descent and return doesn't need to be as arduous as the one devised by the women in this book, *Return to Inanna.*

There are many ways to construct this ritual. Be careful not to take it too literally – feel free to change the number of gates and attach different meanings or colors to them. Use your own symbolism, associations and meanings. I based the gates of my imaginal ritual on both the original Inanna myth and the Hindu system of seven chakras and their associated rainbow colors. There are other symbolic systems that lend themselves to the idea of gates. Think of Dante's circles or Angeles Arrien's *Eight Gates of Wisdom.*

The women's intention in *Return to Inanna,* is to identify and let go of ideas, habits or assumptions that no longer serve them, and to replace the empty space left behind with more beneficent attributes. Every gate represents a different lens through which to examine themselves. In real life, undertaking this kind of introspection at every gate would take at least a week and require a grueling amount of energy, self-examination and dedication.

Instead, participants might pick just *one* habit, belief or assumption to work on. The group or facilitator could then create a question or practice for each gate in which the descent focuses on ways to help release old behavior; the ascent, on embracing change.

You could create an Inanna based ritual with an entirely different intention. For example, I once created a ritual for a Grief Group. I added two further stages (shock and guilt) to the Kubler-Ross five-step model of the grieving process (denial, anger, bargaining, depression and acceptance).

It could be a ritual of initiation into a new profession, a graduation, a divorce or a birth. All such occasions involve releasing old ways of being and creating new techniques and parameters with which to meet the challenge of a change in lifestyle.

I wish you many blessings in creating your own Inanna-based rite of descent and return. In case this process is new to you or you need a little help, I'm including a set of calls for seven directions and an invocation to the goddess Inanna. If you wish, use only four directions – east, south, west and north. Traditions vary widely!

Call to Seven Directions for a Ritual Based on the Myth of Inanna's Descent and Return to the Underworld

Author's Note: I chose to call on four animals connected with the goddess Inanna in art and literature. I set them in the direction which seemed to best fit their own attributes to the respective qualities traditionally associated with east, south, west and north. Please use them at will.

EAST

Standing in a circle, the entire group turns to face east.

Standing in the East, we hail the rising sun, welcoming the inspiration of a new day dawning. We call on the spirit of Mountain Goat, who stands sure-footed on the steepest crags to greet the dawn, senses tuned to whispers in the wind.

May he stand beside us, guide us through our journey, help us pick our way through unknown territory; scaling slopes and descending darkling valleys, ready to taste new ideas, novel thoughts, fresh ways of being.

SOUTH

The group turns to face south.

Standing in the South, we hail the midday sun, welcoming the revelation of full light. We call on the spirit of Lion, who crouches close to ground surrounded by her pride, poised between ease and full attention.

May she welcome us as kin, accompany us into peril, ennoble our hearts and set our spirits ablaze. May she ready us to face the unknown. May we learn from her to devour self-made demons.

WEST

The group turns to face west.

Standing in the West, we hail the setting sun, welcoming the mystic revelations dwelling in the gloaming's liminal light. We call on the spirit of Owl, whose wisdom glides in quietly, blossoms like a moon flower in the far reaches of our minds, trembles on the threshold of consciousness.

May we nestle in his feathers, feel the gentle grasp of his talons lifting us on flights of fantasy and imagination. May he carry us above the landscapes of our dreams and help us to remember the sights and sounds encountered there.

NORTH

The group turns to face north.

Standing in the North, we hail the midnight sun, welcoming the wisdom and comfort inherent in the dark. We call on the spirit of Cow, whose sustenance sustains humankind through untold generations. She is the give-away, every piece and part of her valuable and treasured. Her large heart hears the cries of the world. Her heavy teats hold milk enough to suckle every child. Her paths are sacred, her ways are the ways of love.

May her kindness enfold us. May our spirits find refuge in her abundance. May she teach us to share joyfully, willingly from heart, mind, wisdom and wealth.

ABOVE

The group faces the center of the circle, looking up.

Words fail us as we look Above, to greet an eternity we cannot comprehend. We, who move to the rhythm of the cosmos in a myriad of unwitting ways and from whose dust we are formed, humbly we hail you, blessed by your beauty.

www.christineirving.com

BELOW

The group faces the center of the circle, looking down.

Looking Below we greet our mother, our planet, Earth of our being, the source of all nourishment, the fountain from which all meaning flows. Humbly we greet you, blessed by your beauty.

CENTER

The group faces the center of the circle.

Standing in the Center of our truest selves we greet our own hearts, gift them with truth-telling, gift them with joy. We open ourselves to mystery. We promise our presence and participation in the rite to follow, for the benefit of ourselves, each other and for the well-being of all creation.

Christine's Invocation to Inanna

Blessed Goddess of Darkness and Light,
You who have known lust and sorrow,
tenderness and joy, victory and loss.
Indomitable Lady of ten thousand names,
the Morning Star and Evening Star
who sits beside Moon Mother,
who knows the ways of women.

Come guide us through this journey.
Deliver us into darkness. Hang beside us
as we die to old ways of being. Raise us up
as we struggle along new pathways.
Infuse us with eagerness.

Bless our beautiful bodies.
May our tongues relish flavor.
May our fingers yearn to feel.
May our eyes crave color.
May our ears attune to harmony.
May our noses continue to guide us.
May our limbs long to dance.

Fill us with your power, Inanna.
Lend us your lust for life.
May we learn to live and love what is.

Song to Inanna by Lisa Theil

I am the daughter of the ancient mother,
I am the child of the mother of the world.
(repeat)

Oh, Inanna, Oh, Inanna, Oh, Inanna,

It is you who teaches us
to die, be reborn, and rise again,
Die, be reborn, and rise again,
Die, be reborn, and rise.

I am your daughter, oh ancient mother,
I am your child, oh mother of the world.
(repeat)

Tune:

https://www.amazon.com/Song-to-Inanna/dp/B00750I4CY

Chords: Gm Dm F Bb

https://www.youtube.com/watch?v=hk6gPfD6j48

Lamentations of Dumuzi's sister
2000-1600 BCE
Terracotta Louvre Museum

Lamentation as Public Ritual

O Dumuzi of the fair-spoken mouth,
of the ever kind eyes, she sobs tearfully.
~The Electronic Text Corpus of Sumerian Literature

Dumuzi/Gilgamesh/Tammuz, the golden boy of the
Mesopotamian pantheon, winds through the myths of Inanna as
sibling, suitor, spouse – sometimes ardent lover, sometimes lout.
The tales of these three heroes are thought by modern scholars to
be conflations of the same mythic entity or ancestor. Their tales,
far older than the incredibly ancient clay tablets that contain them,
come to us as a palimpsest of stories, scraped clean and
overwritten time and time again, in which the ghosts of previous
retellings float up to surface, entangled, embedded and impossible
to pick apart.

He was a youthful shepherd god, a sacrificial king, a hero. He
was buff, bold, beautiful, bi-sexual and he died young, though
accounts of his death differ. In the earliest myths, his blood soaks
fallow fields in a permanent paean to fertility; in later ones, he
returns to life.

For thousands and thousands of years his death has been
publicly mourned in the Middle East during a yearly festival of
lamentation. The Babylonian calendar named the month of the
summer solstice after him. His name entered the Hebraic calendar
as the tenth month of the civil year and the fourth month of the
ecclesiastical year. It continues to be the name for the month of
July in the Gregorian calendar as written in Arabic, Syriac and
Turkish.

According to the International Standard Bible Encyclopedia, the
first day of the month of Tammuz is thought to be the day of the
new moon of the summer solstice. The clay tablets of Sumer, the

Akkadian empire and Babylonia record designated days of lamentations for the dead god. The mourning rites of Tammuz are spoken of directly in Ezekiel 8:14 (circa 590 BCE):

> *Then he brought me to the door of the gate of the*
> *Lord's house which was toward the north; and,*
> *behold, there sat women weeping for Tammuz.*
> ~King James Bible

The Hebrew month of Tammuz is also associated with mourning. It is the month when Jews lament the fall of the Temple in Jerusalem, destroyed by Babylonian King Nebuchadnezzar in 605 BCE after a siege beginning on the 9th day of Tammuz and lasting for three weeks.

> *By the rivers of Babylon, there we sat down,*
> *yea, we wept, when we remembered Zion.*
> ~Ezekiel 1:1, King James Bible

Byblos, one of the oldest continually occupied cities in the world, lies on the Mediterranean coast of Lebanon. After Alexander the Great added the city to his empire, Greek culture readily adapted Tammuz into its pantheon, changing his Babylonian name to the Greek, Adonis. Adonis is another slain god, lover of Aphrodite who, like her predecessor Inanna, was a goddess of sensual love.

> *I cry woe for Adonis and say,*
> *"The beauteous Adonis is dead;*
> *and the Loves cry me woe again and say,*
> *"The beauteous Adonis is dead."*
> ~ Bion, *Lament for Adonis*, 2nd Cent. BCE

As late as the 12th century CE, medieval Arab historians noted that women still mourned Tammuz's death on the banks of the Tigris.

The stories change and mingle, incorporating the circumstances and culture of any given moment into the corpus of current myth. Yet one element remains constant – general grief expressed as public mourning.

Lamentation "is an art born of mourning," says Kimberley M. Torres in her thesis paper *Resurrecting Inanna: Lament, Gender,*

Transgression. She expounds on the chaotic nature of grief and contends that the inherent structure of art offers the possibility that the chaos engendered by grief, can in some way be organized and controlled by the art of lamentation.

Communal lamentation can relese an explosive amount of energy in cathartic acts of violent proportion. The promise of catharsis safely contained by a traditional structure, appeals to both the powers that be and the populace they seek to guide, defend or control.

In the west, strong emphasis is placed on reason. Efficiency and tidiness have served to denigrate emotion in an attempt to eliminate the erratic and irrational from daily life. We have lost the art of public lamentation. Gone is the wailing and gnashing of teeth, the rolling in dust, the rending of garments.

This is what Inanna says to Ninshubar when instructing her how to lament Inanna's failure to return from the underworld. It gives us a very clear idea of traditional mourning rituals:

...make a lament for me on the ruin mounds. Beat the drum for me in the sanctuary. Make the rounds of the houses of the gods for me. Lacerate your eyes for me, lacerate your nose for me. In private, lacerate your buttocks for me. Like a pauper, clothe yourself in a single garment...
~ The Electronic Text Corpus of Sumerian Literature

The words seem shocking to modern ears, but ring surprisingly familiar in some parts of our contemporary world. From Calabrian, Nocera Terinese, to Spanish, Bercianos de Aliste, the men of small remote communities in the Mediterranean hinterlands still flagellate themselves during long processions that wind through narrow village streets during the week preceding Easter. Penitents mourn the suffering and death of their savior and regret the failings which necessitated His sacrifice. Even in cosmopolitan Madrid, thousands fill the streets to cry and wail as huge and heavy images of the Pieta, carried by straining men in conical white hoods, parade through downtown streets and avenues, accompanied everywhere by the sound of Marian mantras and the broken sobs of women dressed in deep mourning. On the other side of the world, Pilipino flagellants in Victoria Town also mourn the death of Christ, a young god slain for the spiritual well-being of his people.

Underneath cool exteriors of modernity our atavistic selves remember very well the comfort of mourning in concert and the ecstatic relief that comes from the uninhibited expression of grief's associated volatile emotions – distress, anxiety, pain, helplessness, anger, shame, yearning, loneliness, disbelief, shock, guilt, remorse, regret and the burning desire for retribution.

We witnessed a hint of the power of public lamentation after the death of Princess Diana. *Candle in the Wind*, written by Elton Hercules John* and Bernie Taupin, jumped to #1 in the charts of many countries around the world as soon as it was released, a clear example how art becomes incorporated into ritual lamentation.

The same extemporaneous communal outpouring of grief shows up in the amazing proliferation, across the USA and Europe, of public shrines at places where a person in community has died violently and unexpectedly. Photographs, letters, flowers, candles, and symbolic artifacts representing the deceased, such as badges, stuffed animals, sports equipment, etc., create spontaneous altarpieces as artful and beautiful as any deliberately designed display.

Sometimes fiction conveys the emotional content of an event better than any amount of erudition. Günter Grass' book *The Tin Drum* contains a haunting scene in which Oskar gets hired to play his drum at the Onion Cellar, a nightclub in post-World War II Germany.

At the stroke of midnight, waiters deliver cutting boards, knives and onions to every patron. The people, still numbed by war's aftermath, unable to cry on their own, chop their onions and begin to sob:

---

* I didn't realize Elton John's middle name was Hercules until I researched this article. His name is another example of the persistence of myth. Hercules was the Greek hero who became heir to the tradition of semi-divine heroes represented by Damuzi, Gilgamesh, and Tammuz.

...What did the onion juice do? It did what the world and the sorrows of the world could not do: it brought forth a round, human tear. It made them cry. At last they could cry again. To cry properly, without restraint, to cry like mad. The tears flowed and washed everything away.
~ Günter Grass, *The Tin Drum*

Ancient ritual lamentation practiced since prehistoric times in Mesopotamia, is still extant and thriving in the Middle East. Transfigured by a change in religious orientation, nevertheless it continues to mourn the untimely death of a young hero.

The Shiite month of mourning, Muharram, commemorates the death of Hussein ibn Ali, a grandson of the prophet Mohammed, violently slain in battle near Karbala, Iraq. It seems no coincidence that Karbala lies in the center of the mythic territory of the young Sumerian shepherd king, Damuzi.

Several million people gathered in Karbala this year to attend the twelve hundredth celebration of the current form of this much more ancient rite. The great numbers tell us something about what human beings need to maintain sanity and equilibrium. It speaks to the need for psychic safety nets to relieve the stress of accumulated loss – over 11,000 civilian dead recorded so far this year alone in Iraq.

The long human history of lamentation may well be the expression of an archetypal pattern, inherent in the human psyche, to which we conform unconsciously; rationalizing it later with facts, figures and historical data. It includes song, re-enactments, the carrying of an empty funeral bier or coffin in processions, traditional words and phrases chanted and sung, and some outward physical demonstration of grief, ranging from tears and breast beating to blood-letting flagellation.

The same ritual has endured for 5,000 years of human history and for who knows how many generations during the unrecorded eons that preceded them. However we explain the phenomenon of public lamentation, it continues to endure and find new old ways to manifest among us.

Return to Inanna

Glossary

Author's Note: There are at least three spellings for every Sumerian proper name, I picked the ones that seemed easiest to say and read.

Chakra: Sanskrit word translating as 'wheel' or 'disk.' In yoga, meditation and Ayurveda, seven main chakras align along the spine from tailbone to crown. Each chakra is the focal point of a swirling wheel of vital energy where matter and consciousness meet and meld. Called *Prana*, this invisible force keeps us vibrant, healthy and alive.

Cara: Inanna's hairdresser, manicurist, singer, beautician.

Channeling: the process of allowing one's self to be used by a spirit or being from another realm to communicate across space and time for the purpose of imparting information.

Cuneiform: the earliest form of alphabetical writing yet to be discovered, comprised of slender wedge-shaped characters pressed into wet clay with a reed stylus. Beginning as a system of accounting, it developed into a literary written language that remained in use for three thousand years before being replaced by the Phoenician alphabet.

Damuzi: consort of Inanna, sent to the underworld in her place for failing to mourn her demise. Tammuz in Babylonia, he is also conflated with the more ancient Gilgamesh.

Electronic Text Corpus of Sumerian Literature: makes accessible, via the World Wide Web, more than 350 literary works composed in the Sumerian language in ancient Mesopotamia (modern Iraq) during the late third and early second millennia BCE. The corpus includes Sumerian texts in transliteration, English prose translations and bibliographical information for each composition. The transcripts and the translations can be searched, browsed and read online using the tools of the website.

Enheduanna: (2285-2250 BCE) first known author and poet in written history, high priestess to Inanna and daughter of Akkadian/Sumerian king, Sargon the Great. She is the world's first poet in history whose name we know; best known for three powerful hymns to the goddess Inanna, *Inninsagurra, Ninmesarra,* and *Inninmehusa,* which translate as 'The Great-Hearted Mistress,' 'The Exaltation of Inanna' and 'Goddess of the Fearsome Powers'. Her forty-two more personal poems connect us powerfully across millennia to an ancient people, whose legacies continue to influence us as embedded living memes in contemporary cultures.

Enki: elder god, possibly Inanna's father who rescues her from death in the underworld.

Enkidu: mythic wild man of the forests as opposed to the more domesticated Gilgamesh of flocks and fields. Enkidu starts as a fierce rival of Gilgamesh, but later they become friends and probably lovers, becoming a template for the "buddy" motif still popular in contemporary plots of books and movies.

Ereshkigal: Queen of the Underworld, Inanna's elder sister, the pregnant widow of her recently deceased husband Gugalanna. Ereshkigal blames Inanna for her husband's death.

Galla or gala: problematic term which refers to the *kurgarra* and *galatur* - instinctual, asexual creatures created by Enki to be Inanna's saviors, but also to the word for priestesses and priests of Inanna and also of the demons who escort Inanna from the underworld.

Geshtinanna: the sister of Dumuzi, sister-in-law to Inanna, Ereshkigal and Utu. She pleads to take Damuzi's place in the underworld and is granted the right to replace him for half of each year.

Gilgamesh: believed to be an ancient, possibly sacrificial, king of Sumer who evolved into a semi-divine heroic shepherd, a pastoral deity and prototypal hero, sometimes conflated with Damuzi and Tammuz, all lovers in the myths of the goddess Inanna.

Grok: a word coined by American writer Robert A. Heinlein for his 1961 science fiction novel *Stranger in a Strange Land*, meaning "to understand intuitively or by empathy, to establish rapport with."

Gugalanna: the Bull of Heaven, consort to the Queen of the Underworld, Ereshkigal and controlled by the Lord of the Sky, Anu. In *The Epic of Gilgamesh*, Inanna, spurned by Gilgamesh/Damuzi, demands that Anu release the Bull of Heaven to wreak havoc on the shepherd's pastures in retribution for his insult. The Bull of Heaven is killed by Gilgamesh/Damuzi and Enkidu, widowing his pregnant queen, Ereshkigal, Inanna's sister.

Gyre: as a verb - whirl; gyrate. As a noun - vortex, spiral.

Inanna: Queen of Heaven, ancient Akkadian/Sumerian goddess of sexual love, fertility, war and political might. She is the precursor of Ishtar and Aphrodite, but many times more potent in the range of her powers.

Mesopotamia: refers to the land lying between the Tigris and Euphrates rivers as they flow through parts of modern day Iraq, Syria and Turkey. *Meso* (between) *potamia* is a Greek word meaning *between rivers*. It has also been referred to as "the island" and the Fertile Crescent.

Nana: Sumerian Moon Goddess. Inanna's mother.

Neti: Ereshkigal's gatekeeper, who collects and returns Inanna's powers as she passes through the seven gates of the underworld.

Ninshubar: Inanna's confidant, fellow warrior, trusted handmaiden, friend.

Pala: Sumerian/Akkadian. An esoteric and metaphysical term directly associated with the materialization and dematerialization phenomena. "When she entered the seventh gate, the *pala* robe, the garment of ladyship, was removed from her body." Perhaps the *pala* robe was a garment that allowed the person wearing it to move invisibly or alternatively to be magically transported from place to place.

Sumer (su:mər): established in southern Mesopotamia, during the Chalcolithic and Early Bronze ages, is one of the world's first civilizations, along with ancient Egypt and the Indus Valley civilization.

Utu: the Sumerian sun god, brother to Ereshkigal and Inanna, his twin. Utu was the god of the sun, justice, application of law, and the lord of truth.

Bibliography

Echlin, Kim, Inanna: *From the Myths of Ancient Sumer*, Groundwood Books; August 19, 2003

Campbell, Joseph, *The Hero with a Thousand Faces*, New World Library, 2008.

Demetriou, Helen, *The Courtship of Inanna and Dumuzi*, You Tube, Aug 30, 2010
https://www.youtube.com/watch?v=4wcfl4ziB6s

Demetriou, Helen, *Hail Inanna! Queen of Heaven!* You Tube, May 13, 2011 https://www.youtube.com/watch?v=IP7oopcc6zg

Di Micele, Alice, *Circle Of Women*, Merry Meet, 25 March 2015
https://www.youtube.com/watch?v=N-rWiFyAUnE

Faculty of Oriental Studies, University of Oxford, *Electronic Text Corpus of Sumerian Literature*, Oxford University Press, 2003, 2004, 2005, 2006 The ETCSL project, http://etcsl.orinst.ox.ac.uk/

Hallo, William W. and Van Dijk, J.J.A. *The Exaltation of Inanna*, Yale University Press, 1968

Meador, Betty De Shong, *Inanna, Lady of Largest Heart: Poems of the Sumerian High Priestess Enheduanna*, University of Texas Press, 2000

Meador, Betty De Shong, *PRINCESS, PRIESTESS, POET: The Sumerian Temple Hymns Of Enheduanna*, University of Texas Press, Aug 1, 2009

Notable Women:
https://notablewomen.wordpress.com/

https://notablewomen.wordpress.com/2012/09/11/enheduanna-first-named-author-in-human-history/

https://notablewomen.wordpress.com/2012/09/18/enheduanna-part-2-the-sumerian-shakespeare/

Perera, Sylvia Brinton *Descent to the Goddess: A Way of Initiation for Women,* Inner City Books, 1981

Riccio, Alessio, *NINSHUBAR - From the Above to the Below,* CD , Unorthodox Recordings, May 11, 2013, https://alessioriccio.bandcamp.com/album/ninshubar-from-the-above-to-the-below

Roberts, Janet, *Enheduanna, Daughter of King Sargon Princess, Poet, Priestess (2300 B.C.),* June 08, 2014 http://www.transoxiana.org/0108/roberts-enheduanna.html

Theil, Lisa, *Song to Inanna*, provided to Youtube by CD Baby, ℗ 1994 Lisa Thiel Released October 01, 1994 https://www.youtube.com/watch?v=hk6gPfD6j48

Uktena, Teri, *Inanna's Journey to the Underworld,* You Tube, Jul 23, 2016, https://www.youtube.com/watch?v=QW8n7rCZqoc

Wolkstein, Diane and Kramer, Samuel Noah, *Inanna, Queen of Heaven and Earth: Her Stories and Hymns from Sumer,* Fitzhenry and Whiteside, 1983

Wolkstein, Diane, *Inanna: Her Search for Wisdom*, You Tube, Nov 9, 2011,
https://www.youtube.com/watch?v=HV8vEc0BrdU

Zólyomi, Gábor - Tanos, Bálint - Sövegjártó, Szilvia, *The Electronic Text Corpus of Sumerian Royal Inscriptions*. 2008, last modification: 09 Jul 2016,
http://oracc.museum.upenn.edu/etcsri/index.html

Return to Inanna

About the Author

Christine Irving is ordained in two spiritual traditions. She is a priestess of the Fellowship of Isis, an international spiritual organization devoted to spreading awareness of the Feminine divine, as represented by the ancient Egyptian goddess Isis. Christine has also been ordained into the priesthood of the Gnostic Church of Saint Mary Magdalene. She is a creator and facilitator of ritual, a founding mother of the California Alliance for Women, a Peer Spirit circle guide, and a SoulCollage® facilitator.

Her passion is storytelling in all its myriad forms and she delights in uncovering the perennial wisdom embedded in the world's myths, folk stories and faerie tales. She takes a Jungian view of the world and has made a life-long study of the use and meaning of symbols.

Poetry is her medium of choice, but stories have their own imperative and sometimes demand a longer telling, as in her novel, *Magdalene A.D.* 2012). In 2017 she won first place in The National Federation of State Poetry Societies' annual poetry contest. *Return to Inanna* is her fifth volume of poetry. Her books include *Be a Teller of Tales* (2000), *The Naked Man* (2010), *You Can Tell a Crone by Her Cackle* (2014) and *Sitting on the Hag seat: A Celtic Knot of Poems* (2016).

Christine lives and works in Texas with her beloved husband of fifty years, continually enchanted by the never-ending pageantry of its big skies.

Made in United States
Troutdale, OR
09/06/2023